THIS CANDLEWICK

GAMEBOOK

BELONGS TO:

April

Irene

Eleanor

Pawluk

July/98.

For Richard,
Max, and Molly
C. H.

For Georgia
H. M.

Text copyright © 1996
by Heather Maisner
Illustrations copyright © 1996
by Charlotte Hard

All rights reserved. First U.S. paperback edition 1997

Library of Congress Cataloging-in-Publication Data is available.
Library of Congress Catalog Card Number 96-7354

ISBN 1-56402-878-X (hardcover)

ISBN 0-7636-0136-5 (paperback)

2 4 6 8 10 9 7 5 3 1

Printed in Hong Kong

This book was typeset in Providence Sans.
The illustrations were done in watercolor.

Candlewick Press
2067 Massachusetts Avenue
Cambridge, Massachusetts 02140

SAVE BRAVE TED

Heather Maisner

illustrated by

Charlotte Hard

CANDLEWICK PRESS
CAMBRIDGE, MASSACHUSETTS

HELP! My name is Brave Ted.
My eight friends and I are toys and
we were stolen by Mighty Monster.
He wanted to give us as presents to
the terrible Mini-Monsters who live
at the top of Monster Mountain.

We cut a hole in the
monster's bag to see
which way he went.

Whenever the monster stopped
for a rest, one of us got out and
hid. And we put something else
in his bag.

When we reached Monster
Mountain, the bag was full,
but I was the only toy left.
Mighty Monster was furious!
He locked me up.

I've written down the monster's route for you. Please come and rescue us!

- Follow the route to Monster Mountain.

- Find a toy hiding wherever the monster stopped to sleep.

- Rescue me. Then take us all back home.

Come quickly! Mighty Monster says he may go back and look for the missing toys.

Brave Ted

P.S. I gave this message to Big Brown Bird, who flew with it to you.

Start at the old abandoned church.

Go down the cobblestone path,

past the children with a kite,

around the pond with ducks and swans,

through the yellow gate,

behind the row of smiling cows,

and stop at the basket of apples.

**The monster went to sleep here.
Herbie ran off and hid.
We put some apples in the bag.**

Can you find Herbie?

Now you are going to the forest.

Start at the spot where three fox cubs sit.

Step over two giant spotted toadstools,

go around the bushes with red berries,

to the house with blue window frames,

past a tree where owls live,

between two rows of beehives,

and along the leafy path.

Stop at the pile of logs.

The monster went to sleep here.
Snake slid off and hid.
We put a log in the bag.

Can you find Snake?

Now you are going to the zoo.

Start at the blue arch.

Go past the snake holding
a bunch of balloons,

up to the bridge,

over the pool where
penguins play,

in front of the hippos
in their pond,

between two tigers,

and under the trees
where parrots fly.

Stop at the wheelbarrow
full of bricks.

**The monster went to sleep here.
Percy ran off and hid.
We put a brick in the bag.**

**Can you
find Percy?**

Now you are going to the desert.

Start by the woman
in a dark blue dress.

Go behind a big fish
spraying water,

in front of a man
selling brooms,

over a large tortoise,

around a man charming
a snake,

to a tall prickly cactus,

and past the trees where
camels stand.

Stop at the banana tree.

The monster went to sleep here.
Rosie ran off and hid.
We put some bananas in the bag.

Can you
find Rosie?

Now you are going to the fair.

Start by the clown
in spotted pants.

Go under the snake
roller coaster,

to the crazy mirror,

around the fortune-
teller's tent,

in front of the
ice cream seller,

behind the curvy slide,

and past the coconut toss.

Stop at the mound
of coconuts.

**The monster went to sleep here.
Raspberry ran off and hid.
We put a coconut in the bag.**

**Can you
find Raspberry?**

Now you are going to the river.

Start on the left at the red rowboat.

Paddle through lilies,

between two crocodiles,

under Butterfly Bridge,

behind Monkey Island,

in front of leaping frogs,

beneath the fishing rod,

and past the mermaid sitting on a rock.

Stop by the giant seashell.

**The monster went to sleep here.
Panda ran off and hid.
We put a shell in the bag.**

Can you find Panda?

Now you are going into the sea.

Start at the pink
and orange coral.

Go behind the crab
sitting on a rock,

over the octopus that
lives in a ship,

left to the large
black anchor,

around the place where
starfish dance,

through the waters
where striped fish swim,

and up to the pebbly beach.

The monster went to sleep here.
Puppy ran off and hid.
We put some pebbles in the bag.

Can you
find Puppy?

Now you are going into the cave.

Start where the spider
is spinning a web.

Go under the brown
hanging bats,

around the bones of
a big dinosaur,

past a flickering lantern,

to the sleeping bears,

down a knotted rope,

and across the stones in
a blood-red stream.

Stop at the pile
of jagged rocks.

**The monster went to sleep here.
Elly ran off and hid.
We put a rock in the bag.**

**Can you
find Elly?**

Now you are going to the mountain.

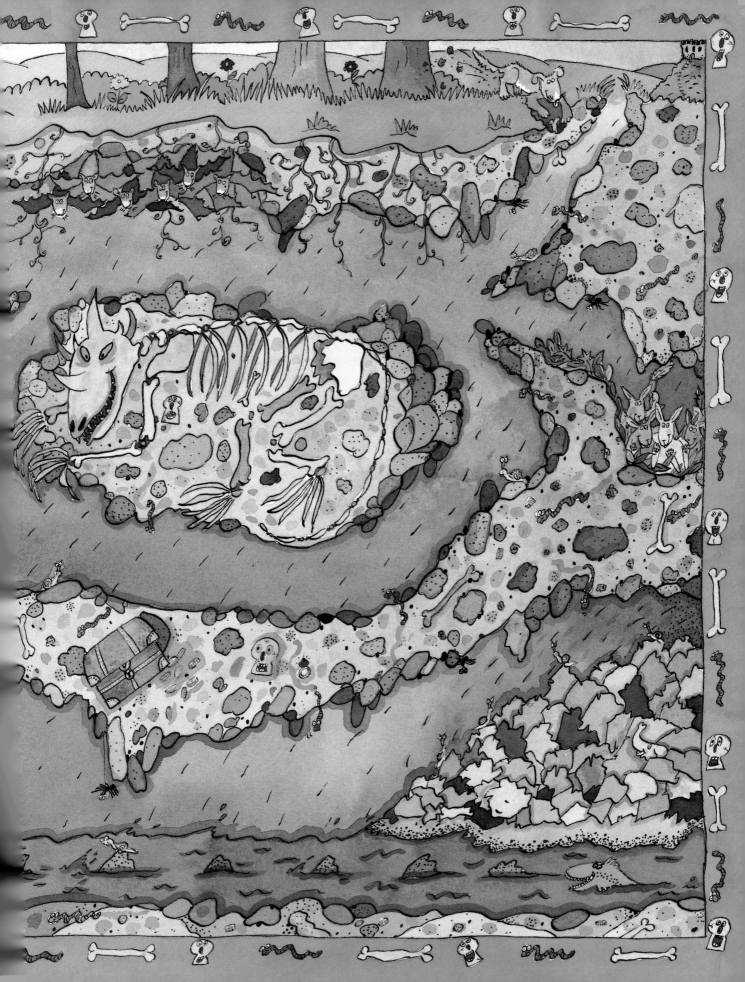

Start by the giant slimy snail.

Go past the scary green plants,

between the flaming monster heads,

under the ghastly floating ghosts,

around a gnarled and twisted tree,

over a bridge across a moat,

through the open rotting door,

and into the castle at the top of

Monster Mountain!

Can you see me?